PIANO • VOCAL • GUITAR

Hillsong UNITED aftermath

ISBN 978-1-4584-0011-6

7777 W. Bluemound Rd. P.O. Box 13819 Milwaukee, WI 53213

For all works contained herein:
Unauthorized copying, arranging, adapting, recording, Internet posting, public performance,
or other distribution of the printed music in this publication is an infringement of copyright.
Infringers are liable under the law.

Visit Hal Leonard Online at
www.halleonard.com

CONTENTS

4   take heart

12   go

20   like an avalanche

27   rhythms of grace

34   aftermath

41   bones

48   father

56   nova

66   light will shine

72   search my heart

82   awakening

Take Heart

Words and Music by
JOEL HOUSTON

Capo 4 (G)

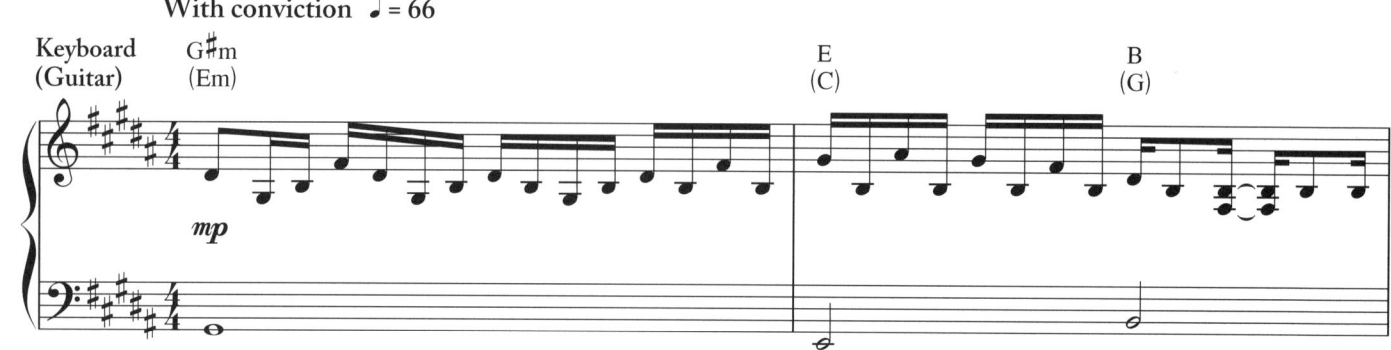
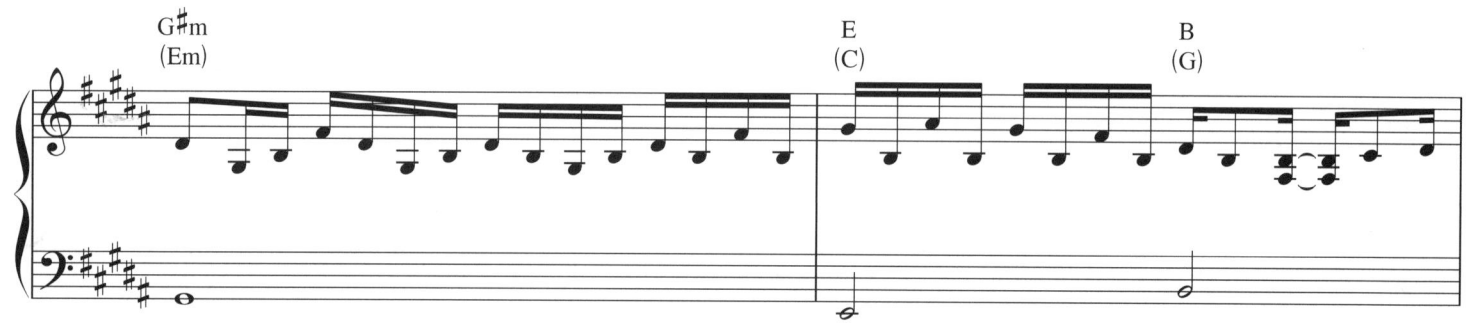
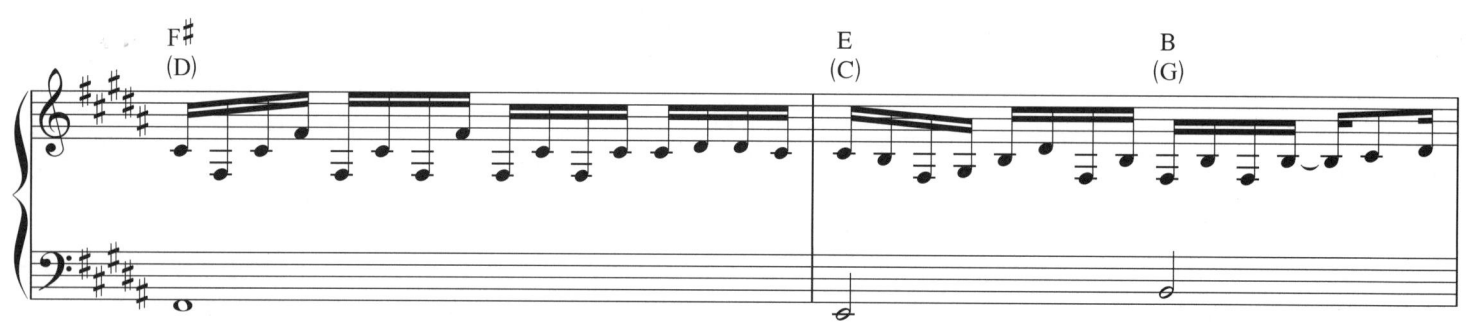
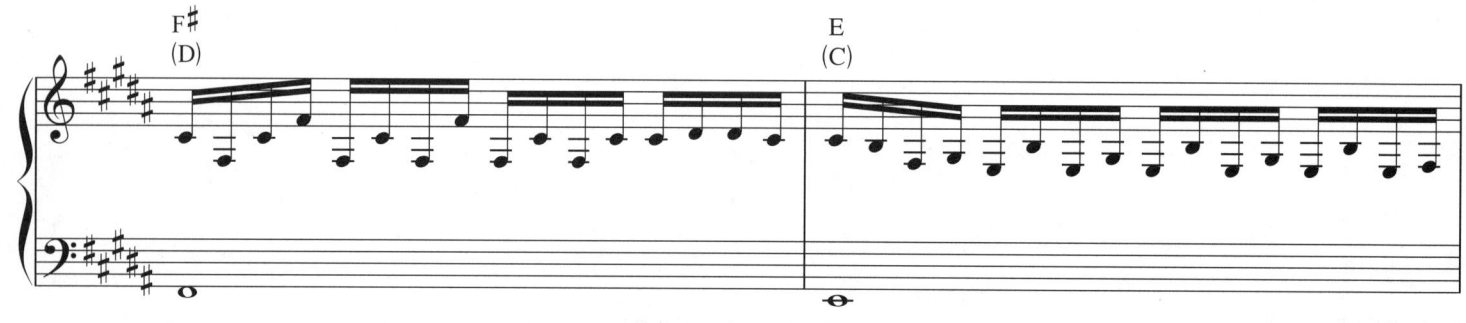

© 2010 HILLSONG PUBLISHING (ASCAP)
Admin. in the United States and Canada at EMICMGPUBLISHING.COM
All Rights Reserved   Used by Permission   CCLI Song No. 5409031

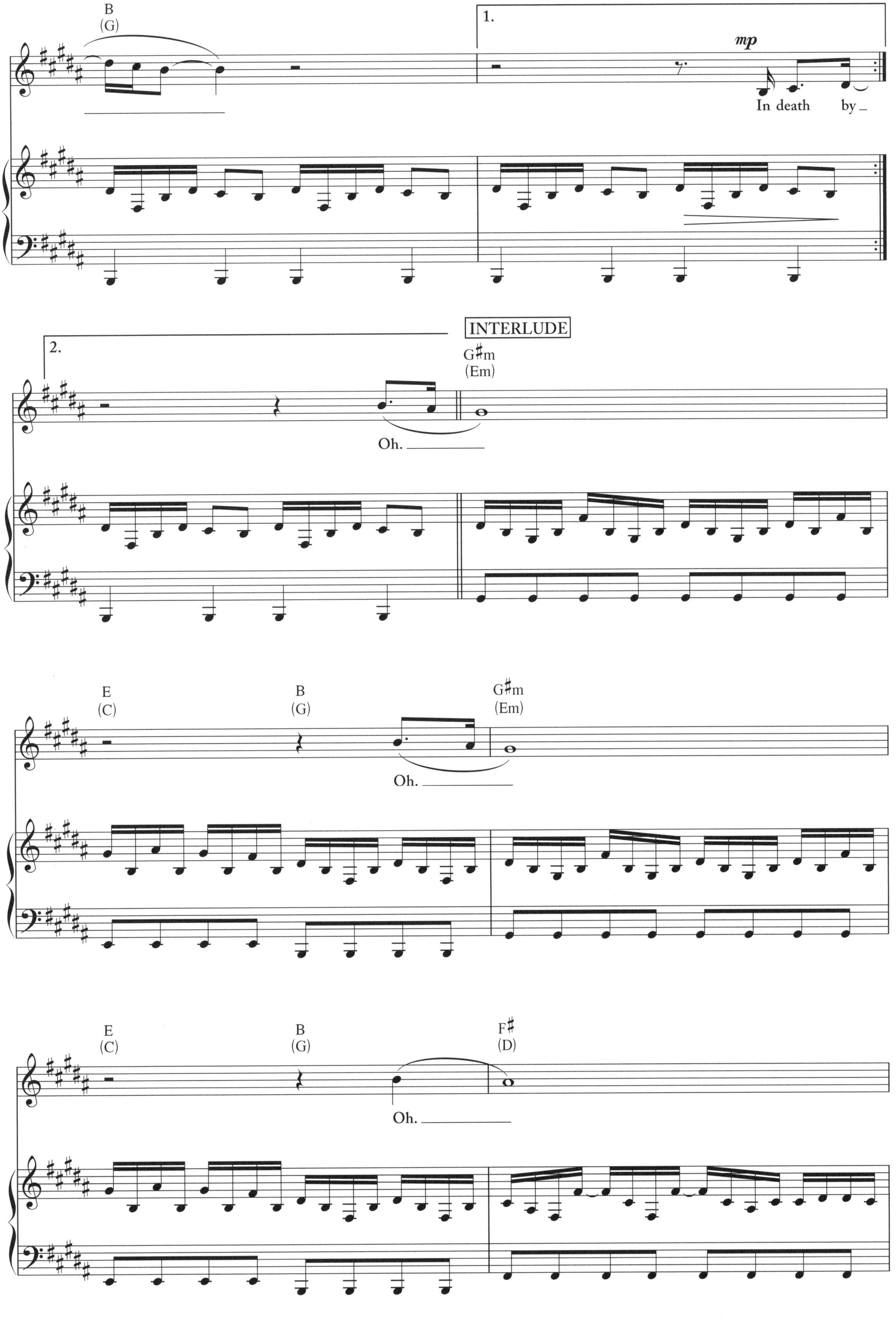
B
(G)
1.
mp
In death by
2.
INTERLUDE
G♯m
(Em)
Oh.
E
(C)
B
(G)
G♯m
(Em)
Oh.
E
(C)
B
(G)
F♯
(D)
Oh.

11

1. G#m (Em) He ___ has o - ver - come. ___

2. G#m (Em) He ___ has o - ver - come. ___

B (G)   C#m (Am)   E (C)   F# (D)

(Vocal 1st time only)

G#m (Em)   B (G)

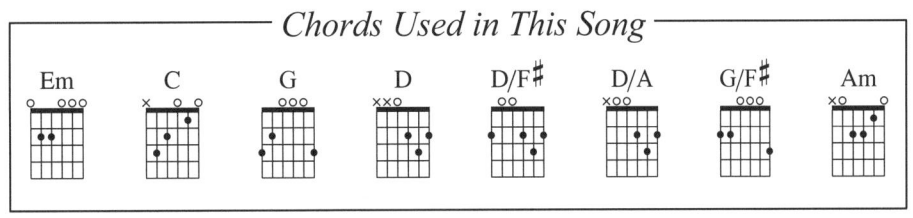
Chords Used in This Song
Em   C   G   D   D/F#   D/A   G/F#   Am

Go

Words and Music by
MATT CROCKER

Capo 4 (G)

With energy! ♩ = 144

CHORUS

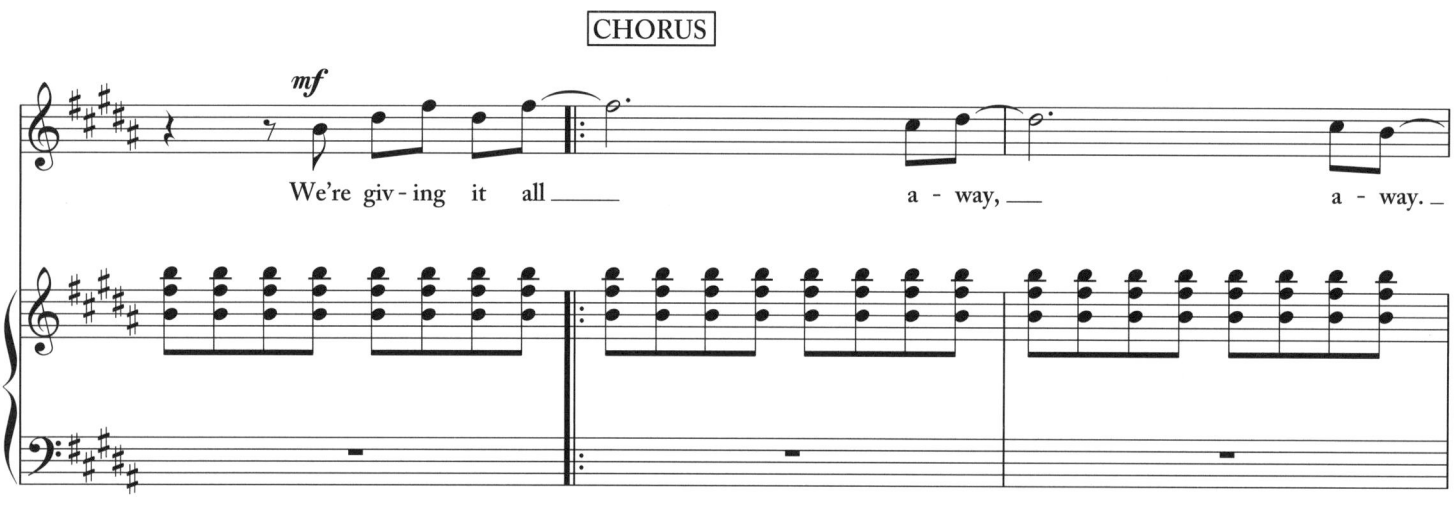

We're giv-ing it all away, away.

We're giv-ing it all to go

© 2010 HILLSONG PUBLISHING (ASCAP)
Admin. in the United States and Canada at EMICMGPUBLISHING.COM
All Rights Reserved   Used by Permission   CCLI Song No. 5806706

*Opt: First time play B chord through entire chorus

19

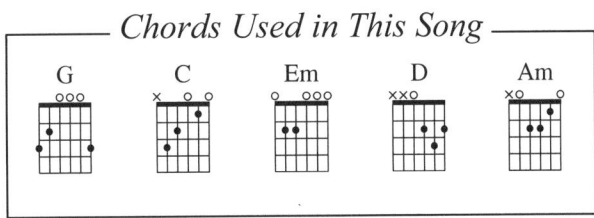
Chords Used in This Song: G C Em D Am

Like an Avalanche

Words and Music by JOEL HOUSTON
and DYLAN THOMAS

Capo 1 (C)

With motion ♩ = 84

[Verse 1] 1. Beau-ti-ful God, lay-ing— Your maj-es-ty a--side. You reached out— in love to show me—

© 2010 HILLSONG PUBLISHING (ASCAP)
Admin. in the United States and Canada at EMICMGPUBLISHING.COM
All Rights Reserved Used by Permission CCLI Song No. 5806713

B♭m
(Am)
D♭
(C)
A♭
(G)
G♭
(F)
mp
B♭m
(Am)
D♭
(C)
A♭
(G)
B♭m
(Am)
D♭
(C)
A♭
(G)
G♭
(F)
B♭m
(Am)
D♭
(C)
A♭
(G)
G♭
(F)

Chords Used in This Song
Am
C
G
F
G/B

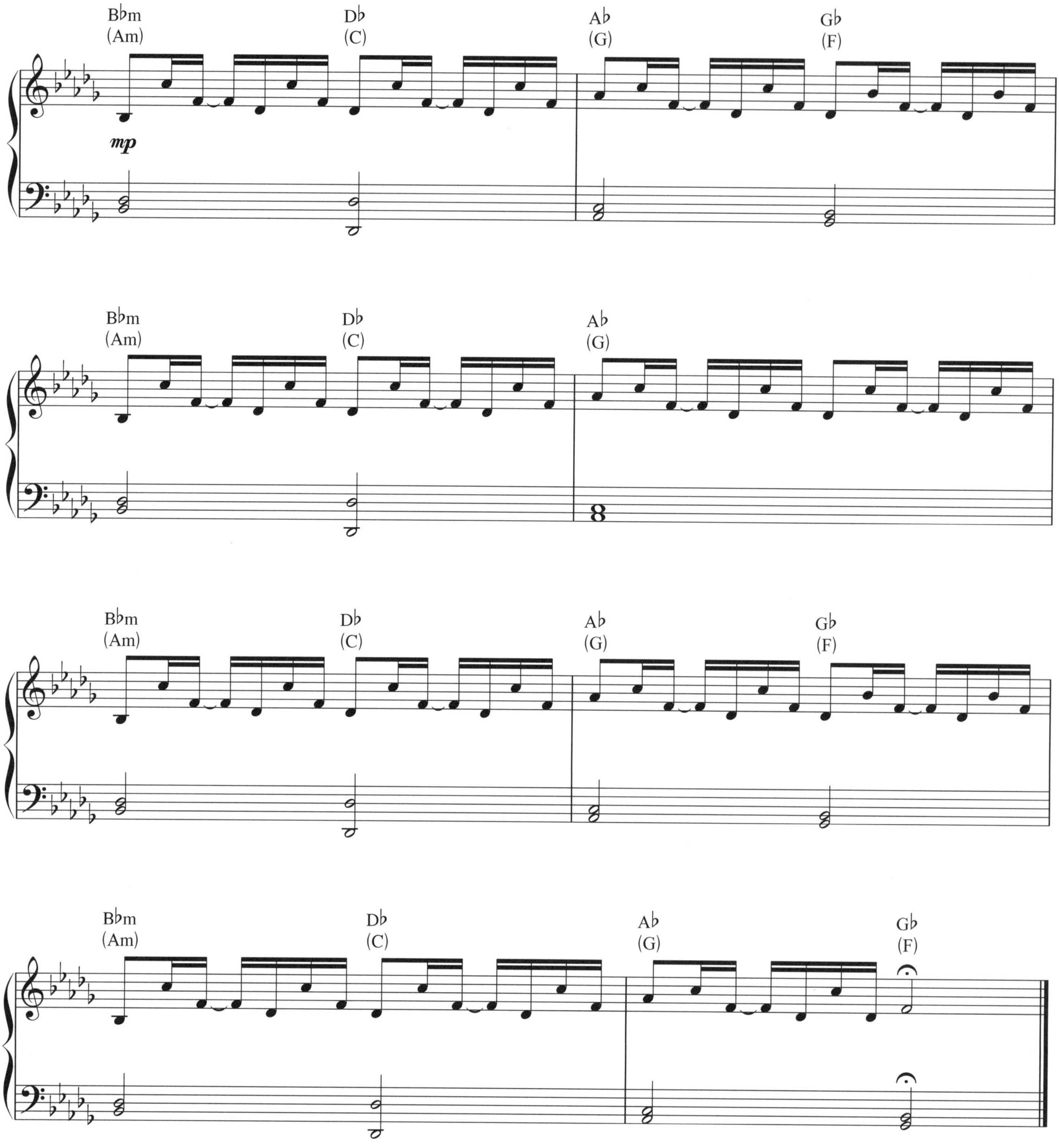

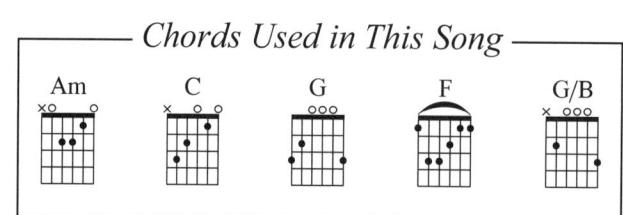

Rhythms of Grace

Words and Music by DEAN USSHER
and CHRIS DAVENPORT

© 2010 HILLSONG PUBLISHING (ASCAP)
Admin. in the United States and Canada at EMICMGPUBLISHING.COM
All Rights Reserved   Used by Permission   CCLI Song No. 5807860

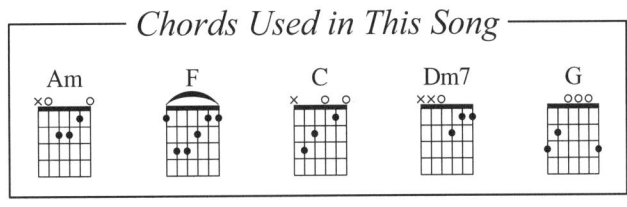

Aftermath

Words and Music by
JOEL HOUSTON

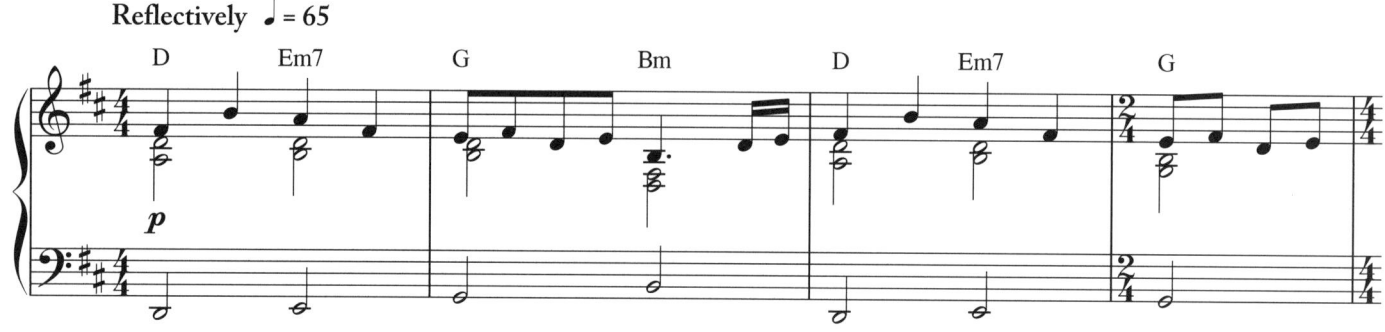

1. The

1. skies lay low where You are. On the earth You rest Your
2. Freedom found in Your scars, in Your grace, my life re-

© 2010 HILLSONG PUBLISHING (ASCAP)
Admin. in the United States and Canada at EMICMGPUBLISHING.COM
All Rights Reserved   Used by Permission CCLI Song No. 5809026

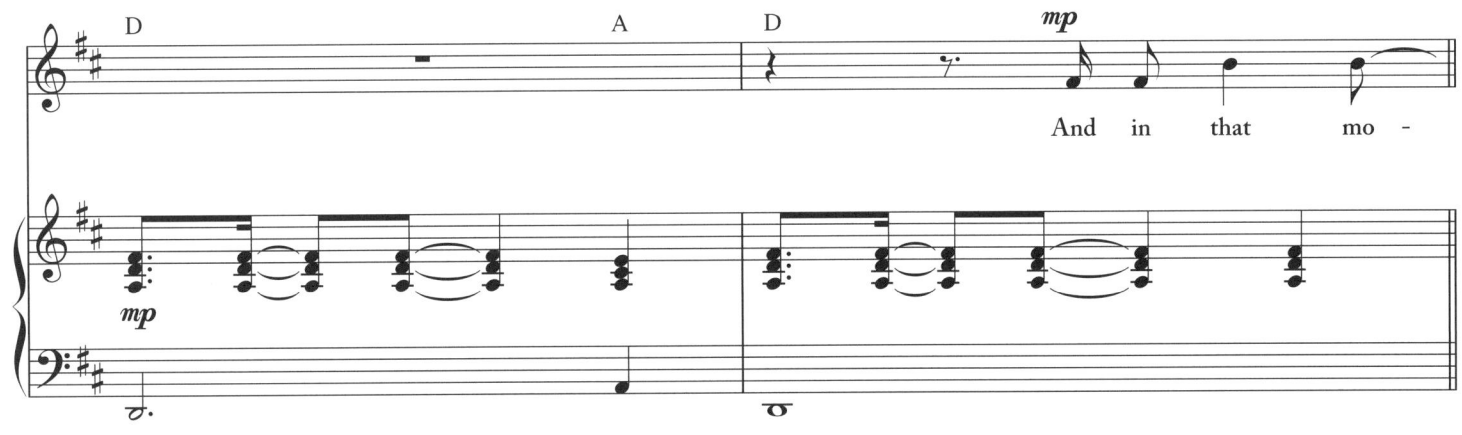
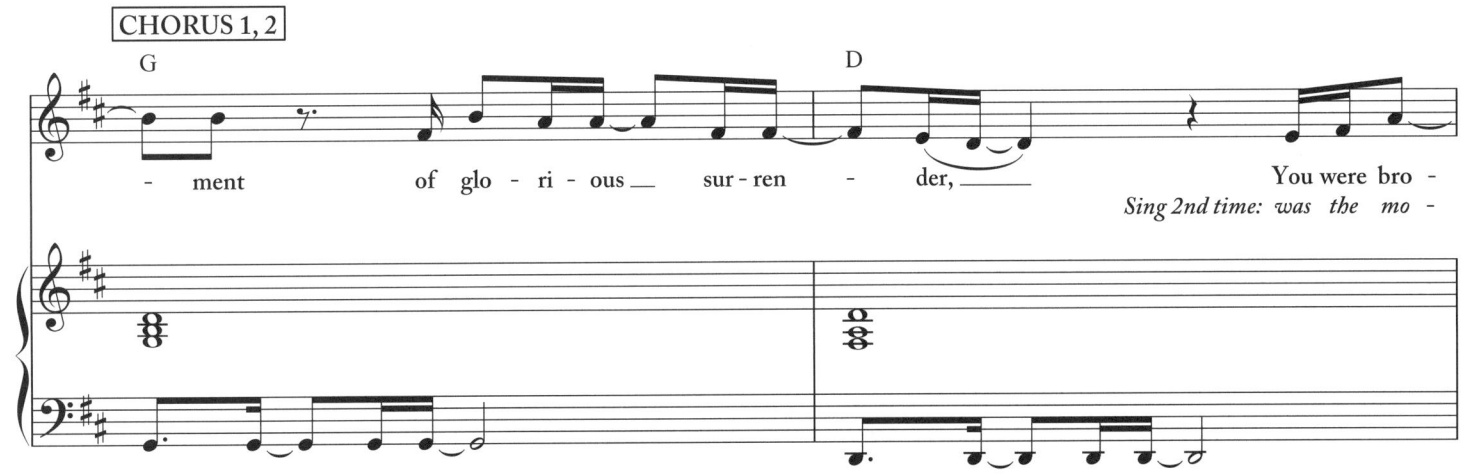

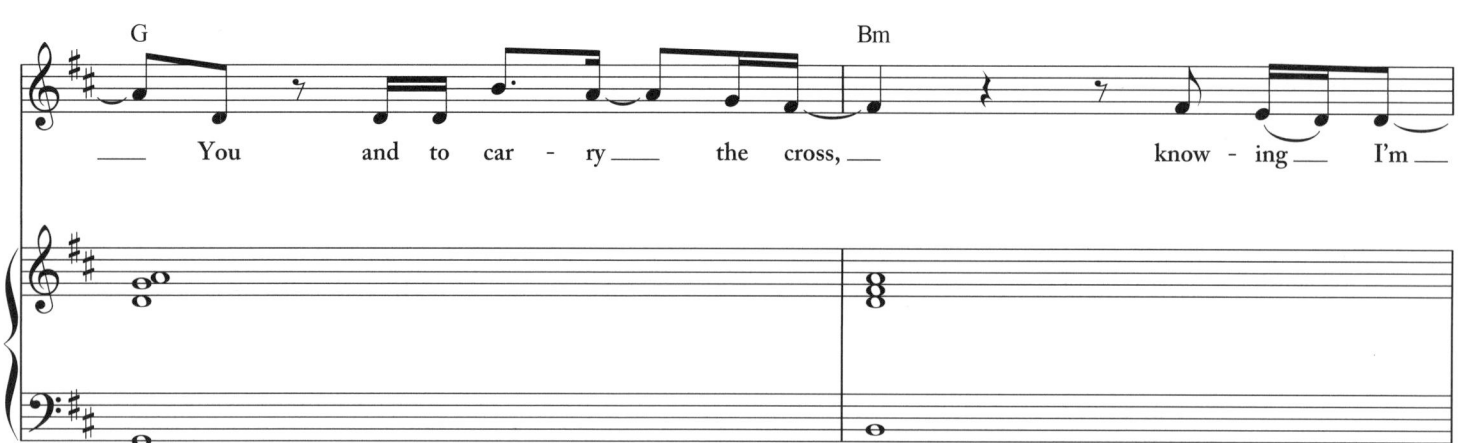
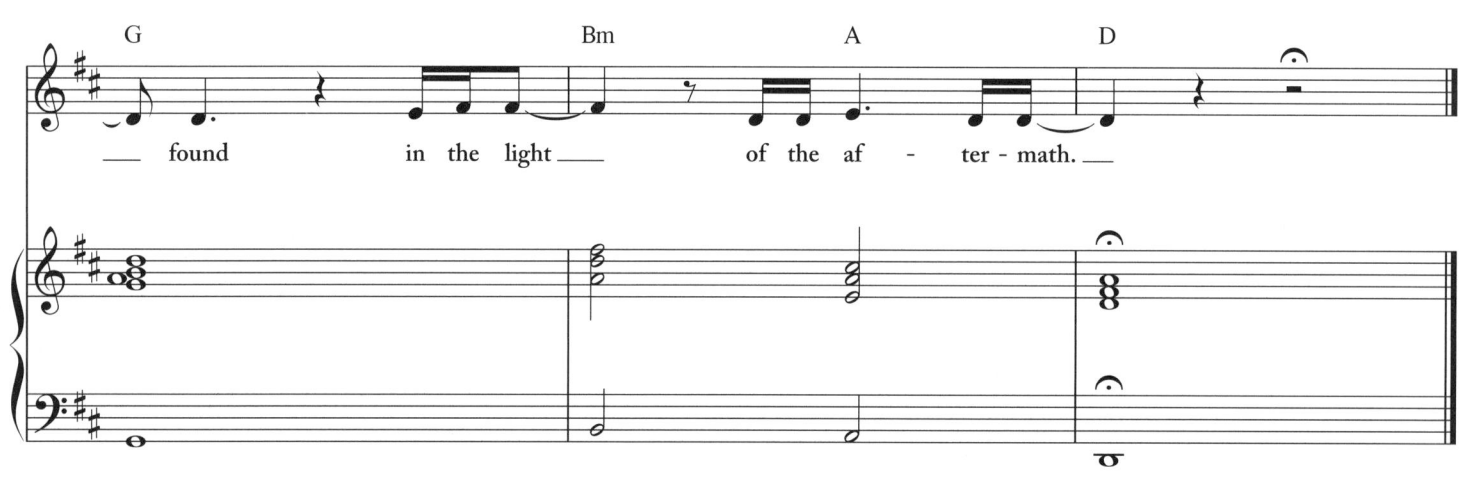
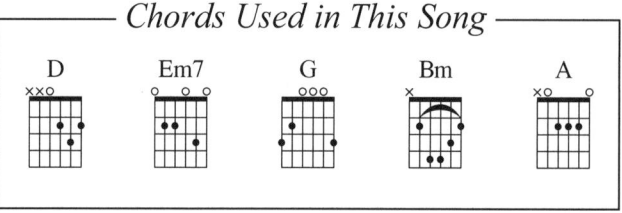

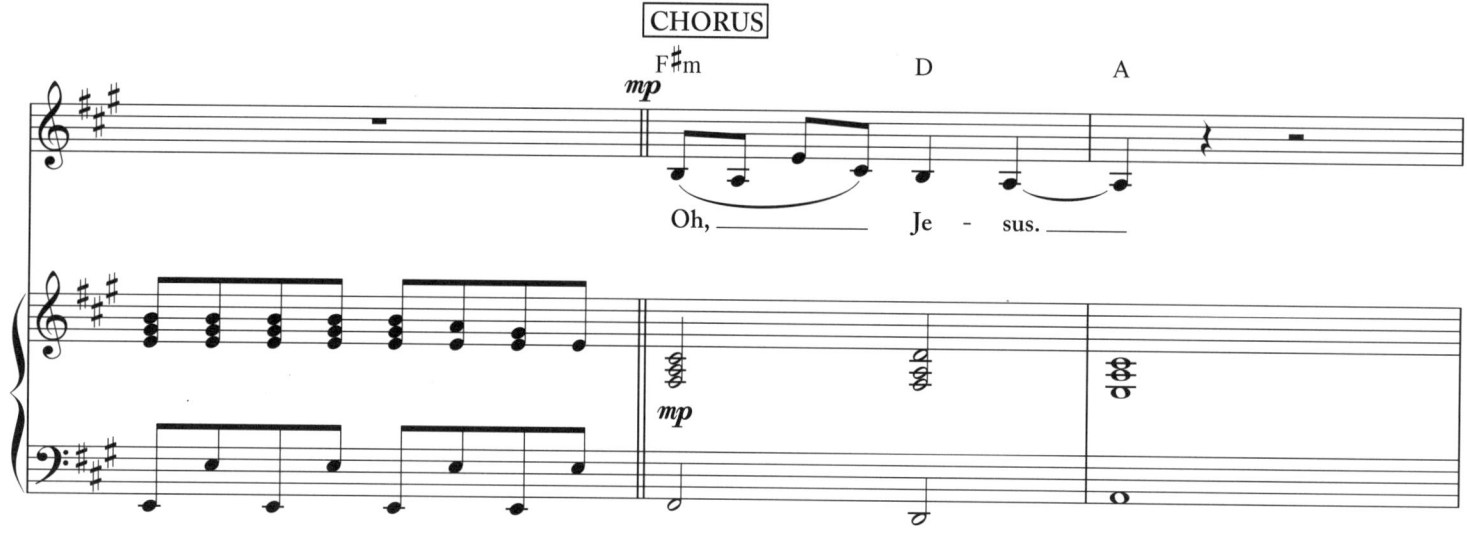

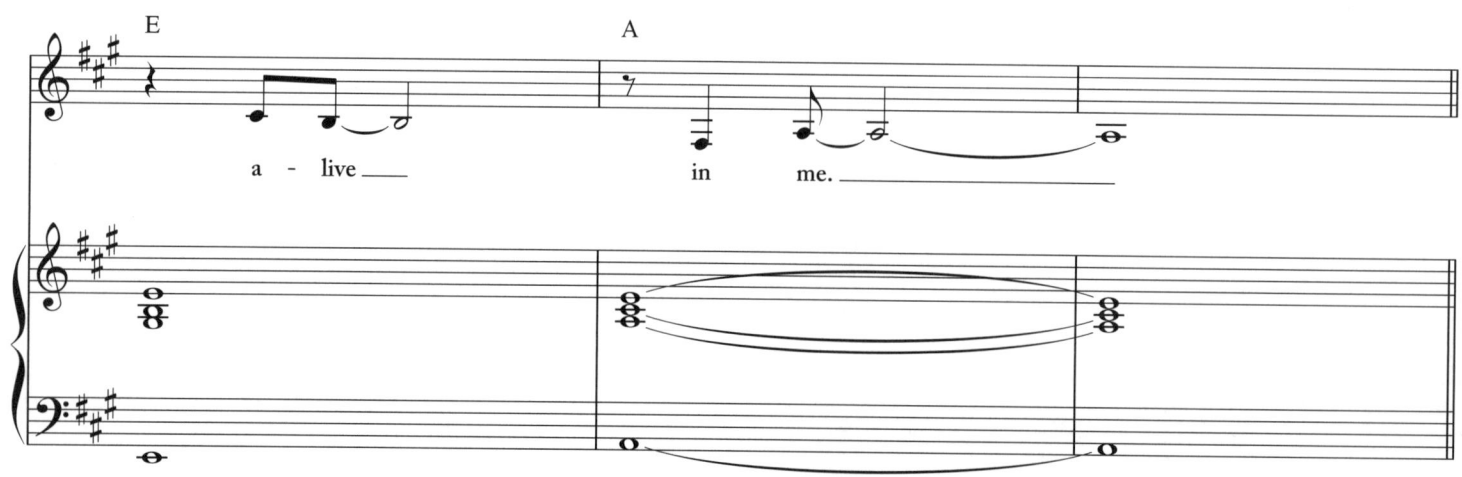

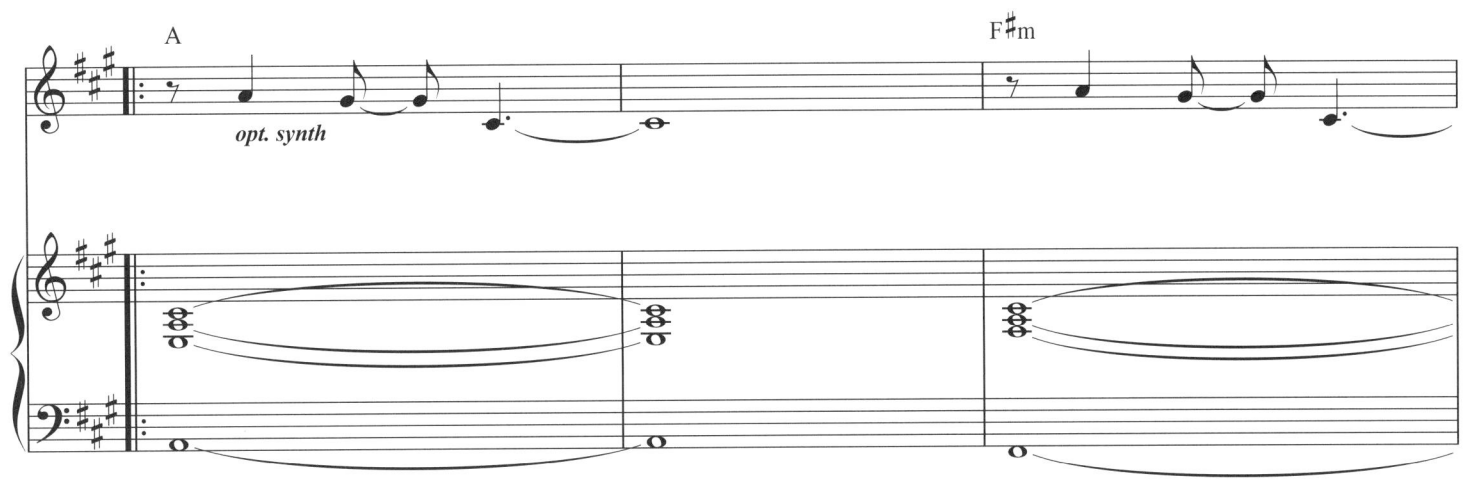

Chords Used in This Song

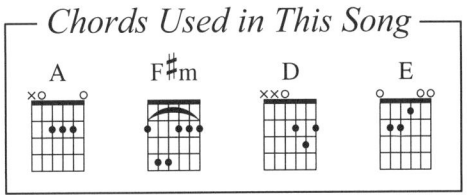

Father

Words and Music by
JOEL HOUSTON

Bm
D
You gave it all for one and all.
G
D
Your grace e-nough, for-ev-er this means
Bm
G
D
Play 3 times
Bm
G
D
love.
(Vocal 1st time only)

Chords Used in This Song
Bm
G
D
Em
A
Asus

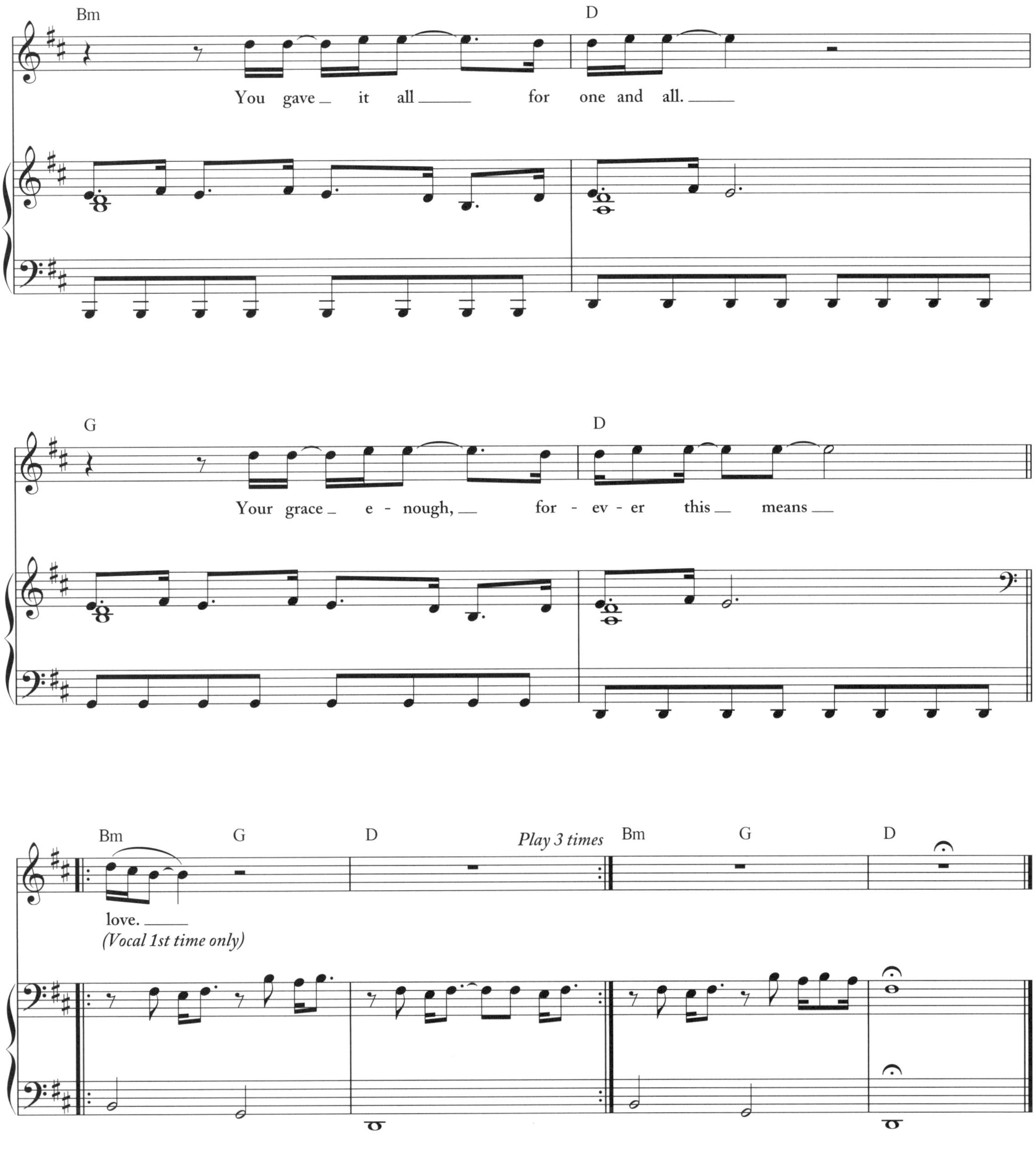

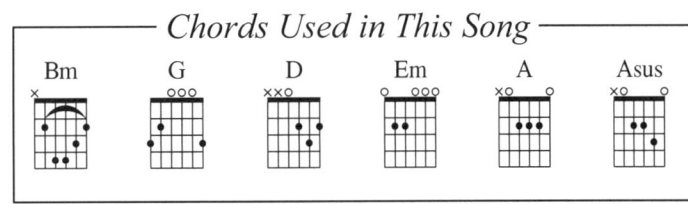

Nova

Words and Music by JOEL HOUSTON,
MATT CROCKER and MICHAEL GUY CHISLETT

Capo 4 (G)

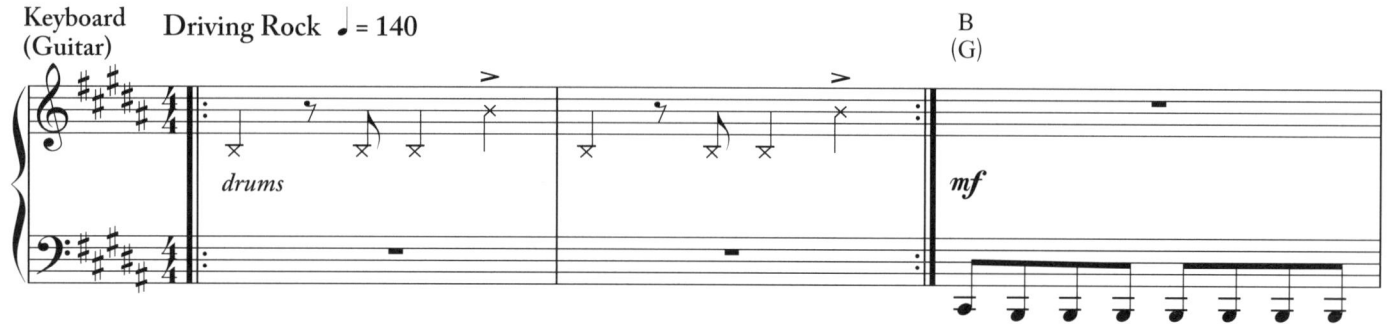

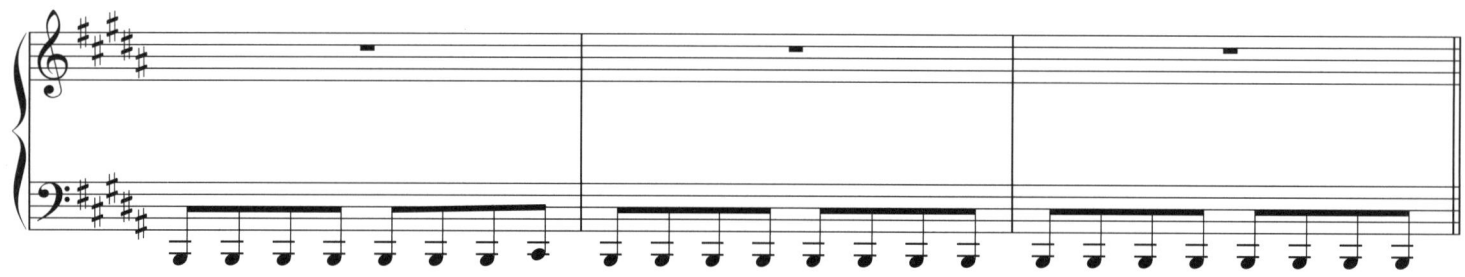

© 2010 HILLSONG PUBLISHING (ASCAP)
Admin. in the United States and Canada at EMICMGPUBLISHING.COM
All Rights Reserved Used by Permission CCLI Song No. 5807891

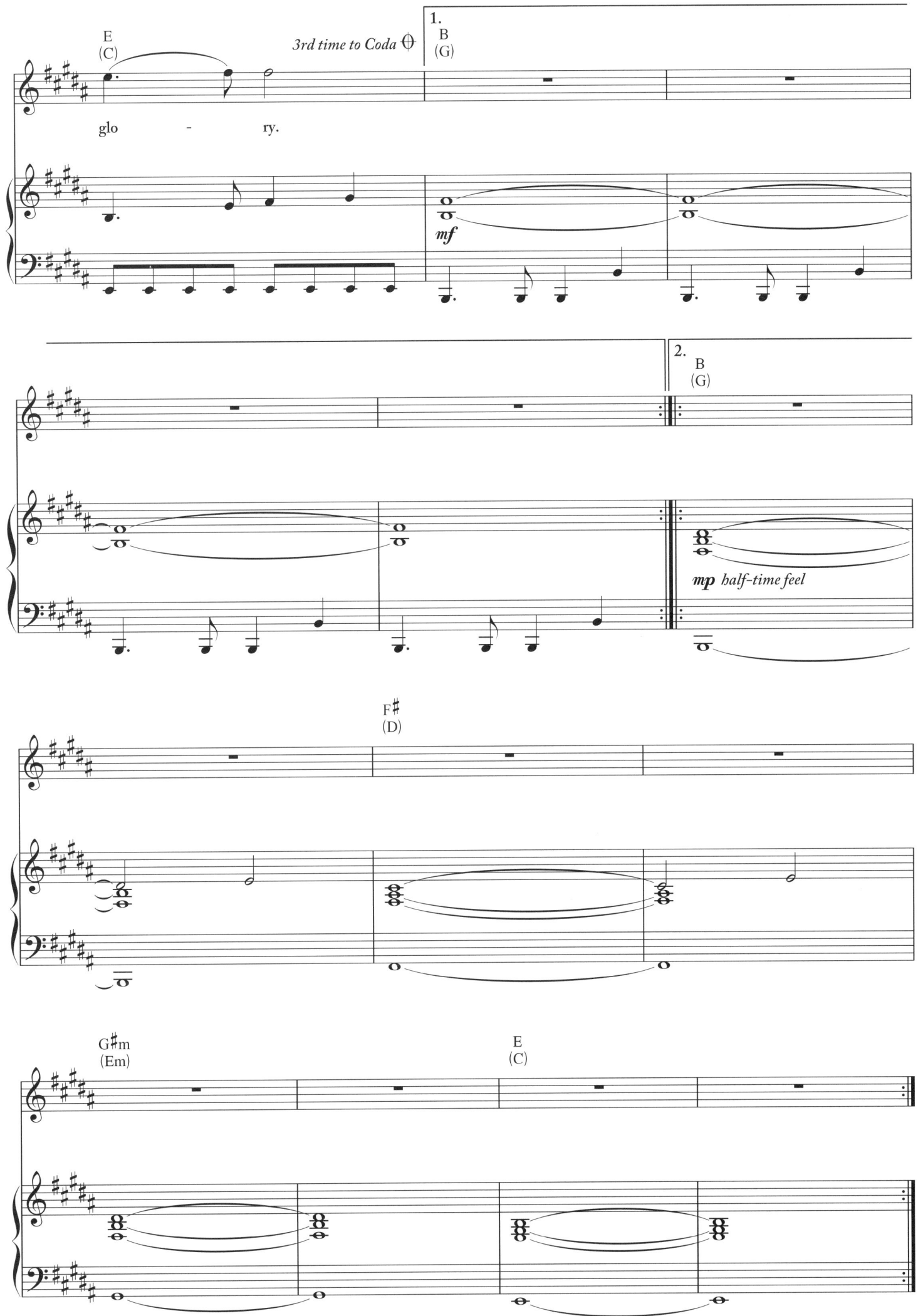

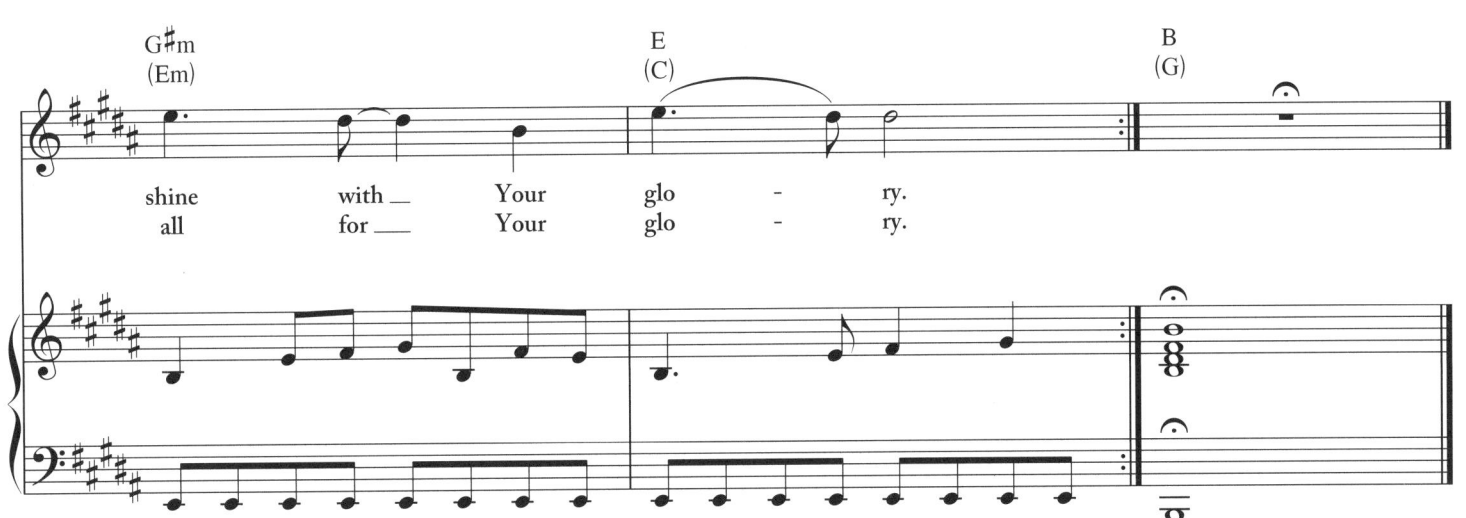
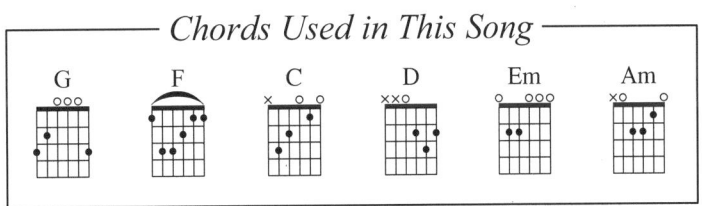

Light Will Shine

Words and Music by MATT CROCKER
and MARTY SAMPSON

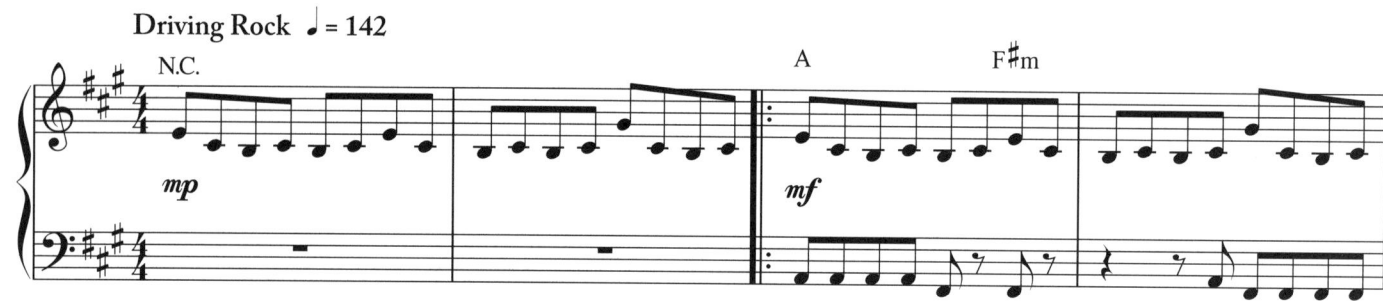

© 2010 HILLSONG PUBLISHING (ASCAP)
Admin. in the United States and Canada at EMICMGPUBLISHING.COM
All Rights Reserved Used by Permission CCLI Song No. 5807901

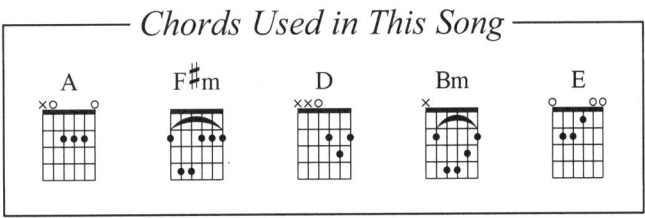

Search My Heart

Words and Music by JOEL HOUSTON and MATT CROCKER

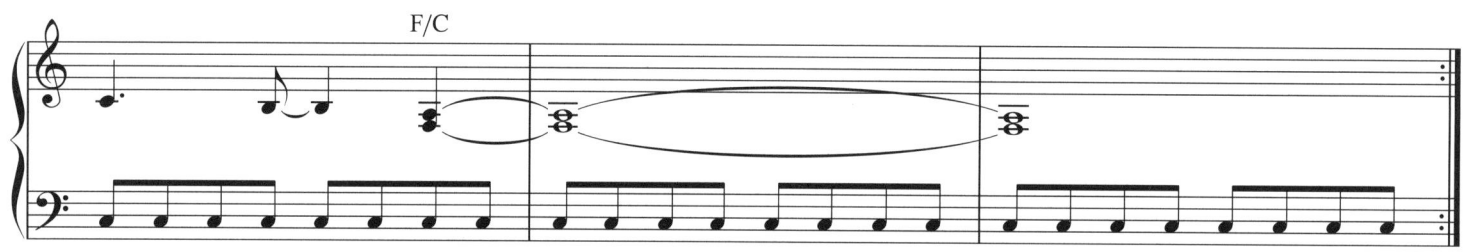
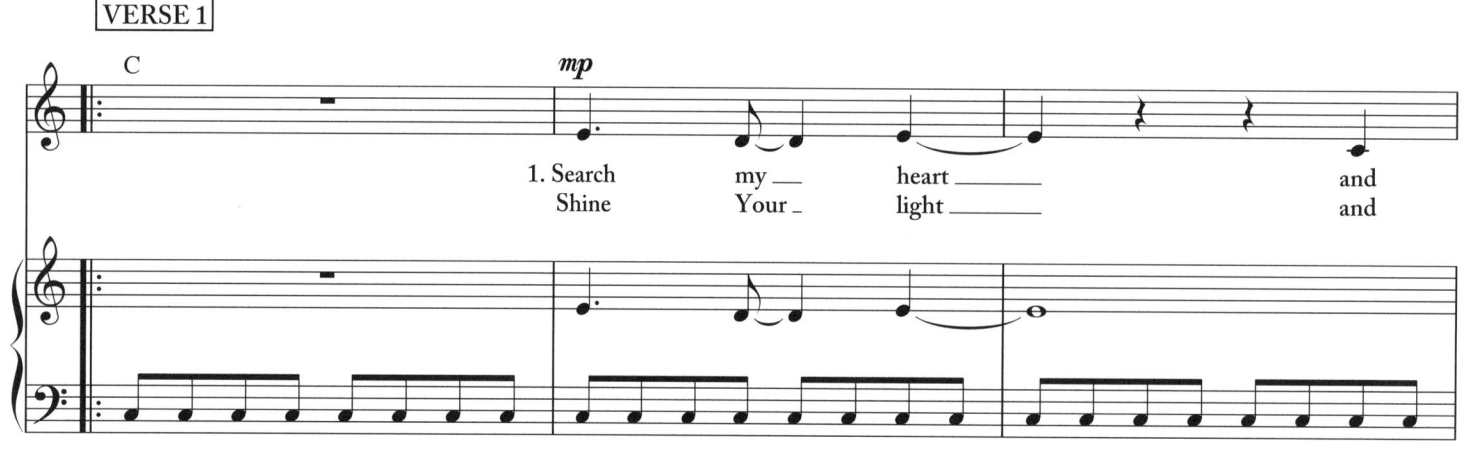
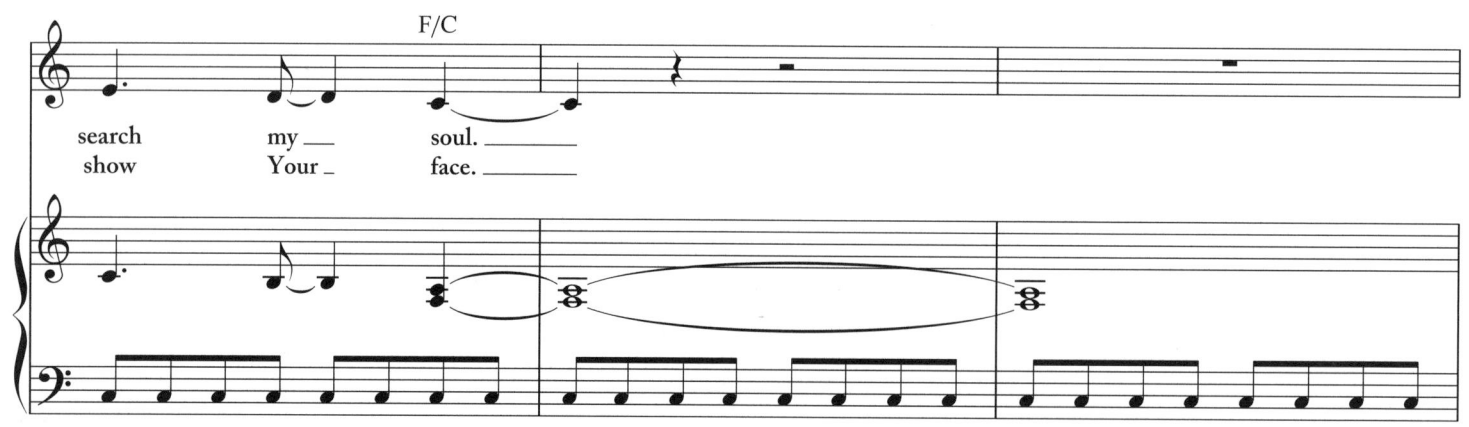

© 2010 HILLSONG PUBLISHING (ASCAP)
Admin. in the United States and Canada at EMICMGPUBLISHING.COM
All Rights Reserved   Used by Permission   CCLI Song No. 5807918

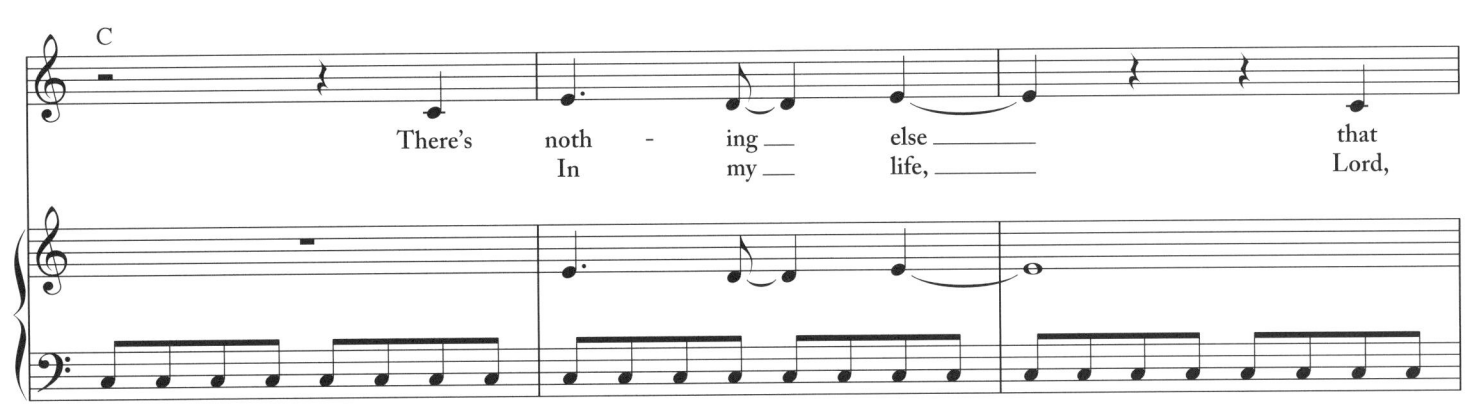
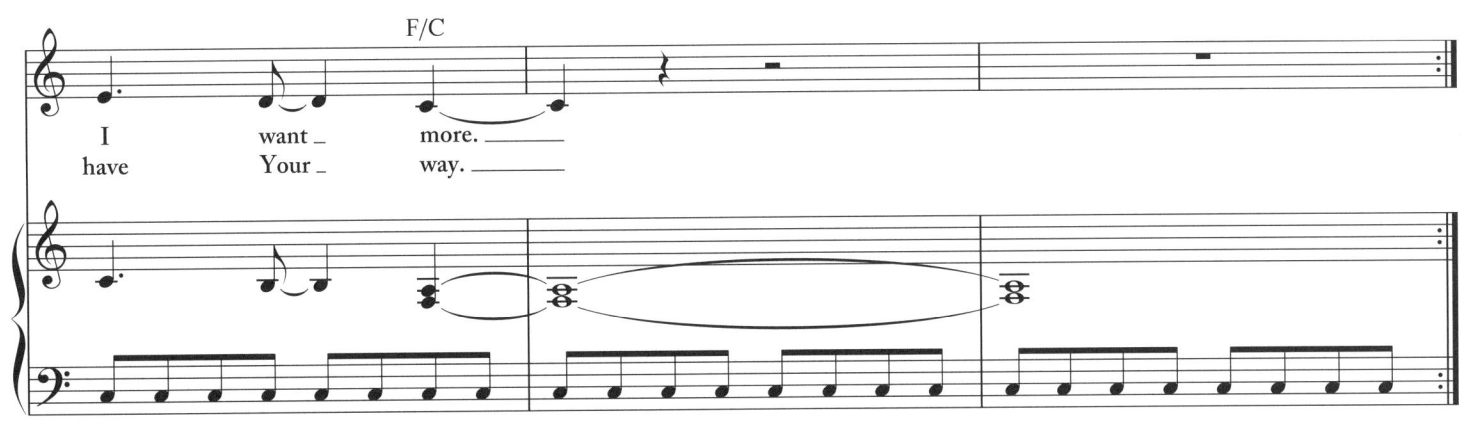

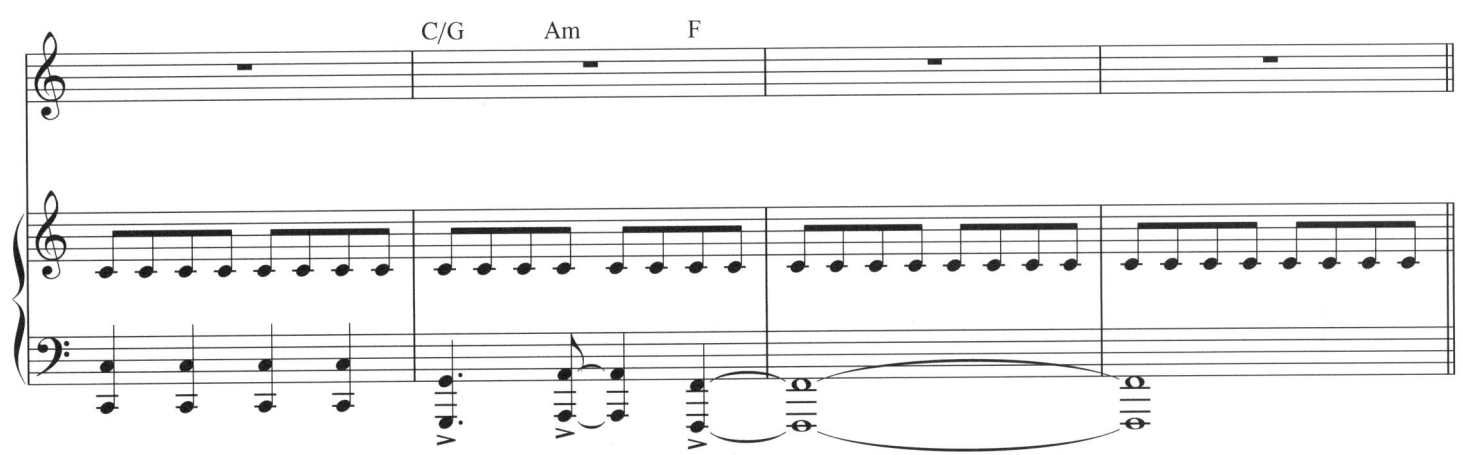

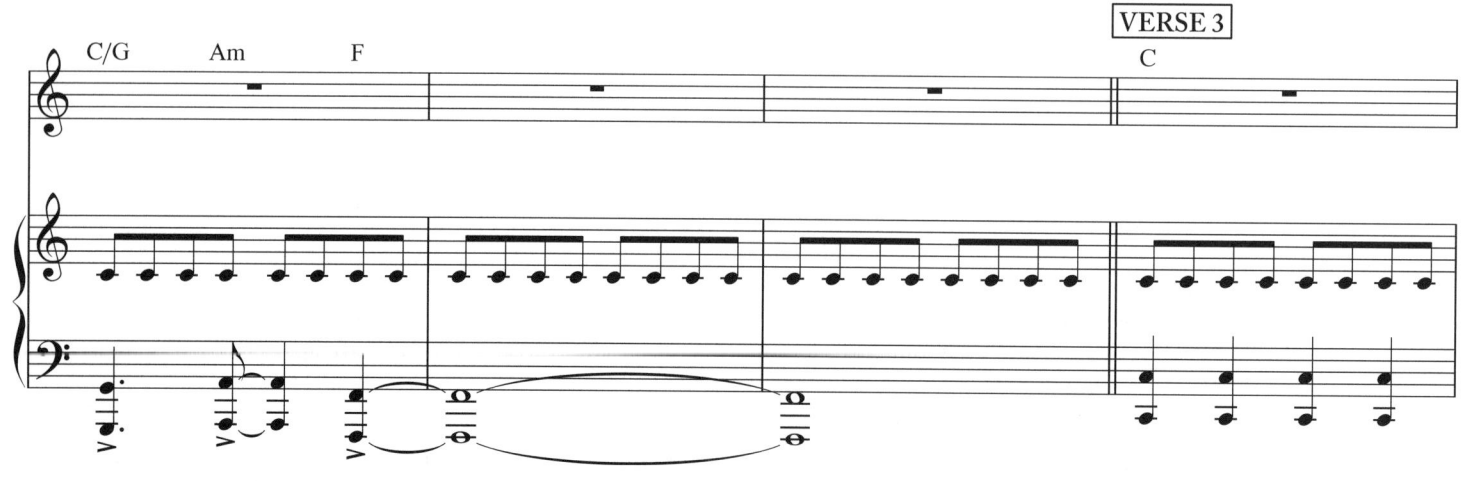

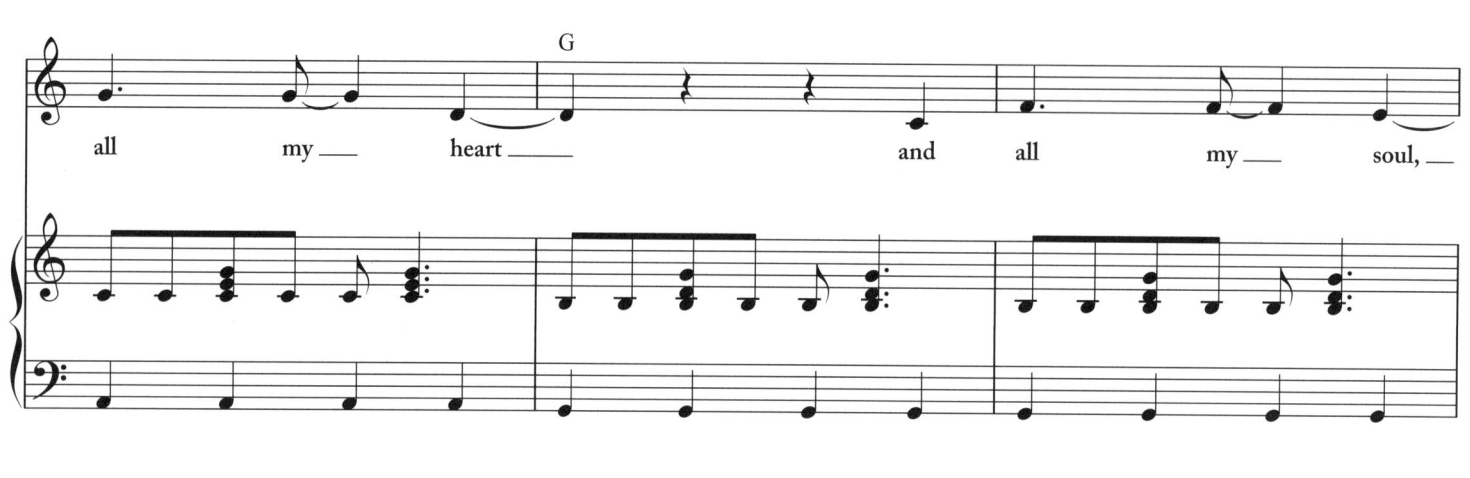

Am
With-out You, I am noth - ing.
F
With-out You,
I am noth - ing.
C
mf
Search my heart
and search my soul.
F/C
mf

Chords Used in This Song
C
F/C
C/G
Am
F
G

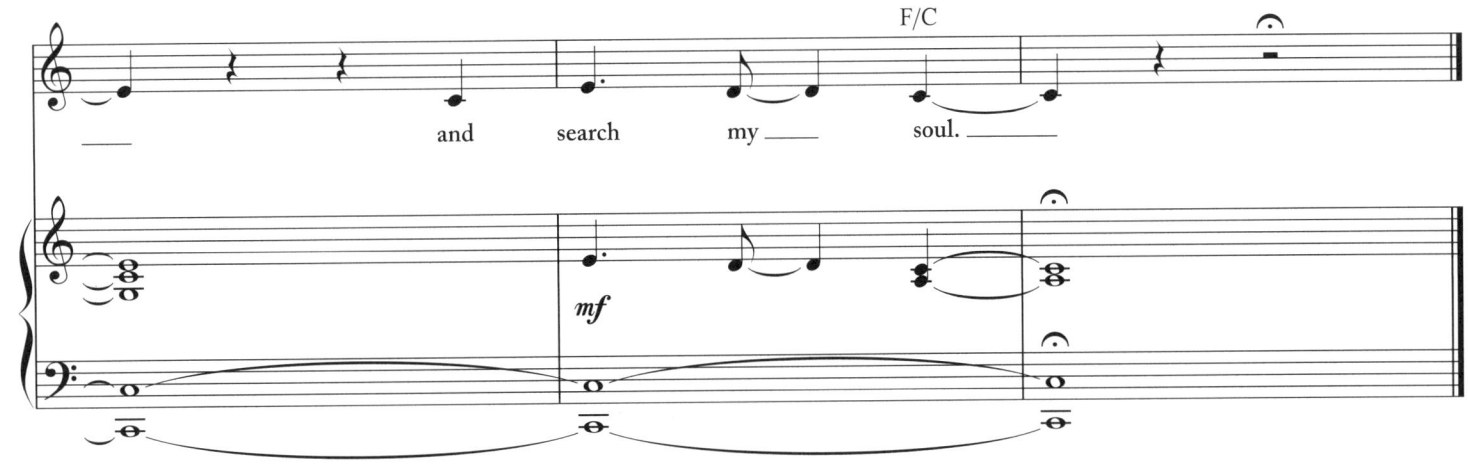

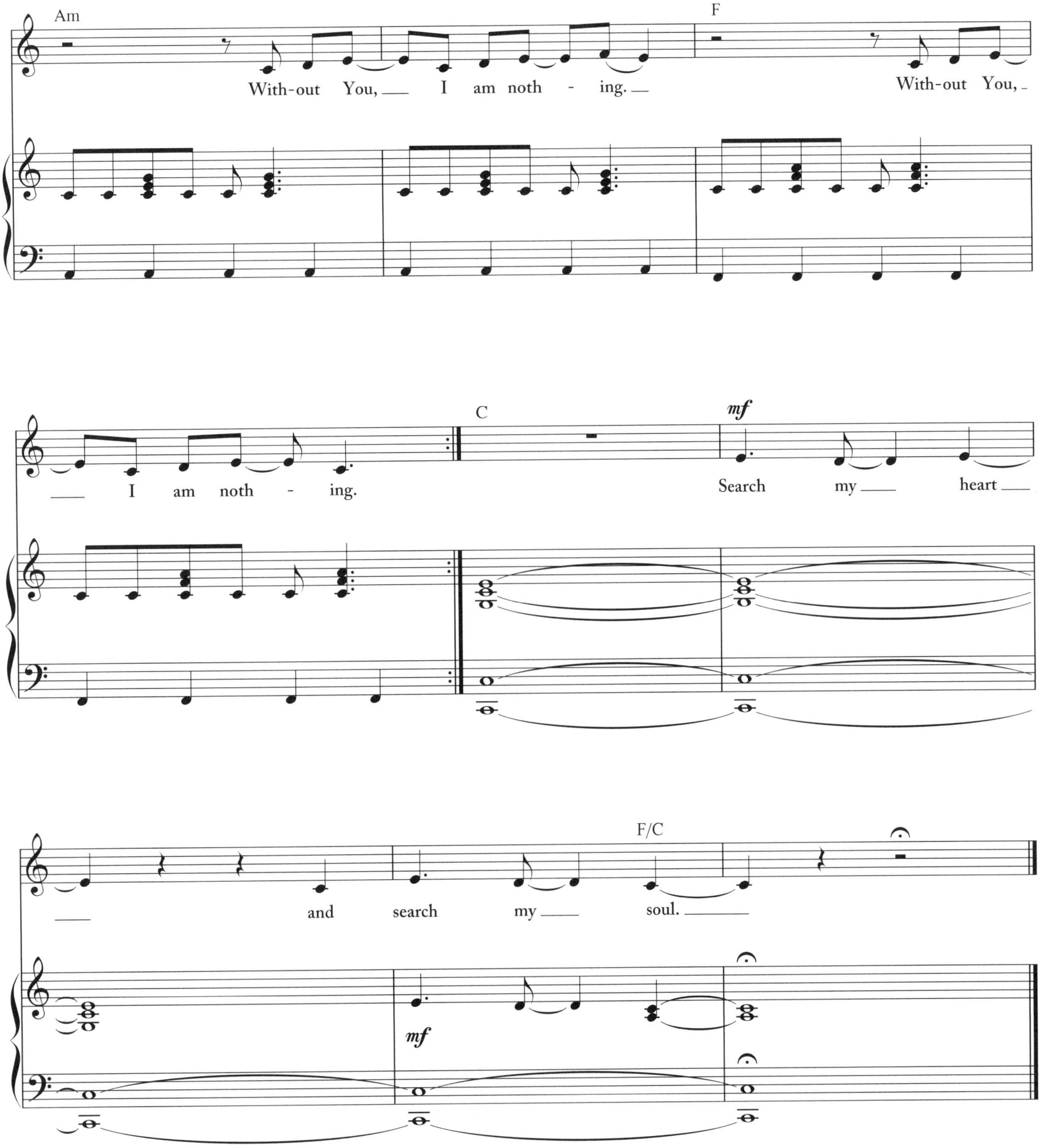

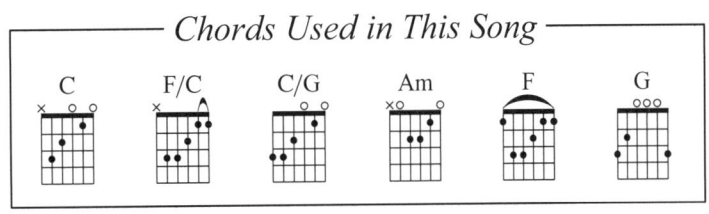

Awakening

Words and Music by REUBEN MORGAN and CHRIS TOMLIN

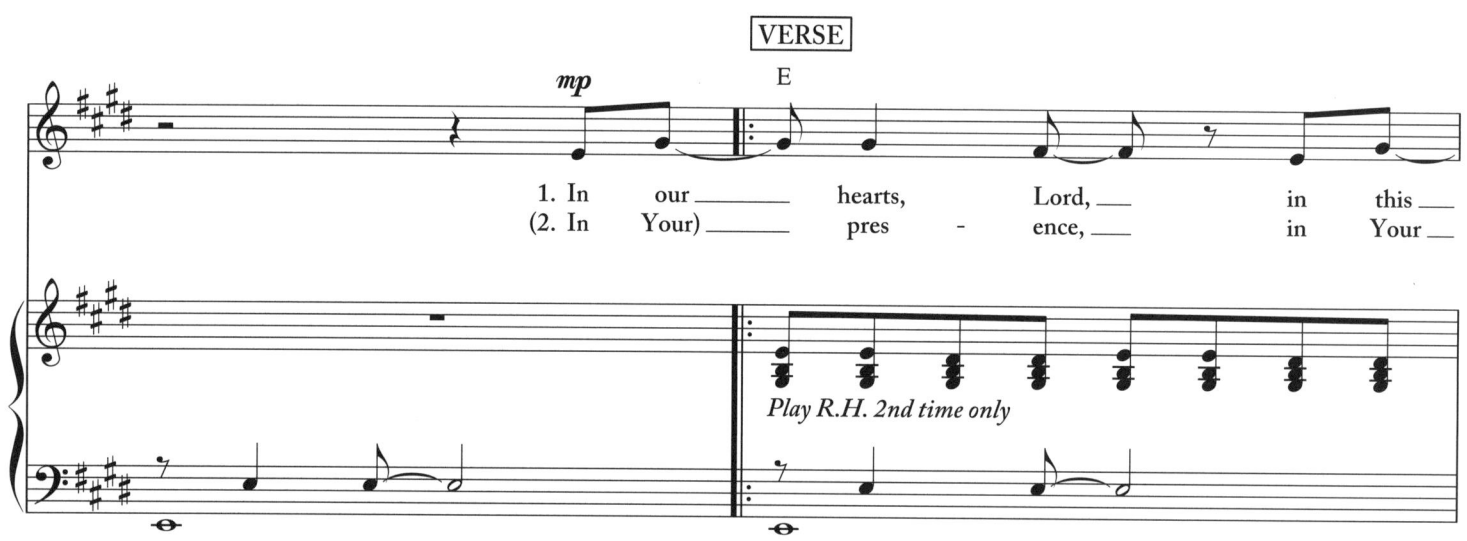
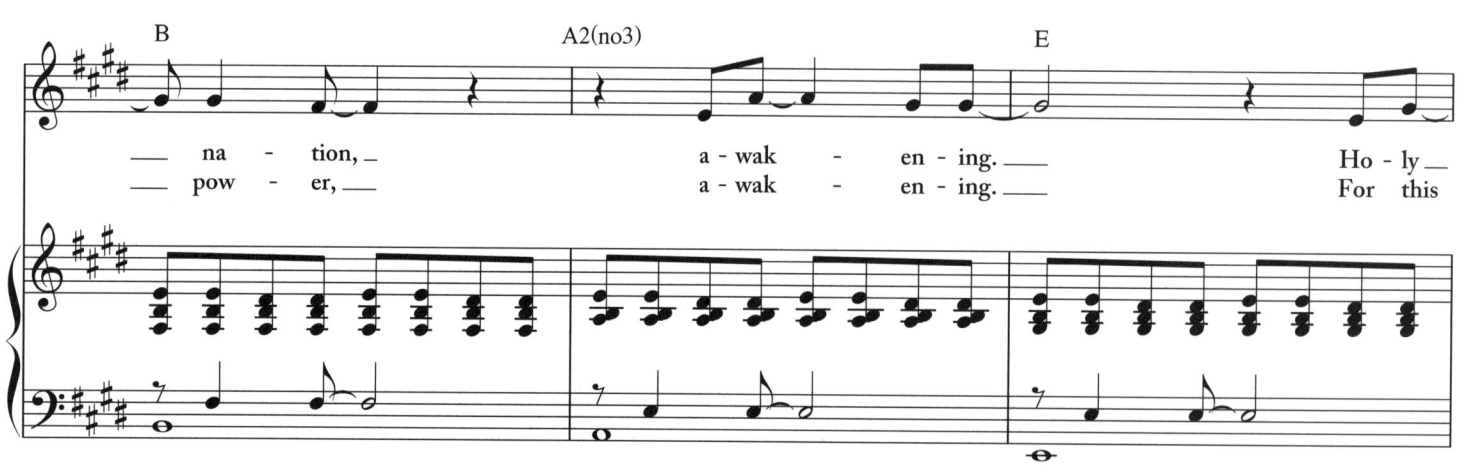

© 2010 HILLSONG PUBLISHING (ASCAP), WORSHIPTOGETHER.COM SONGS (ASCAP), sixsteps Music (ASCAP) and VAMOS PUBLISHING (ASCAP)
HILLSONG PUBLISHING Admin. in the U.S. and Canada at EMICMGPUBLISHING.COM
WORSHIPTOGETHER.COM SONGS, sixsteps Music and VAMOS PUBLISHING Admin. at EMICMGPUBLISHING.COM
All Rights Reserved Used by Permission CCLI Song No. 5677399

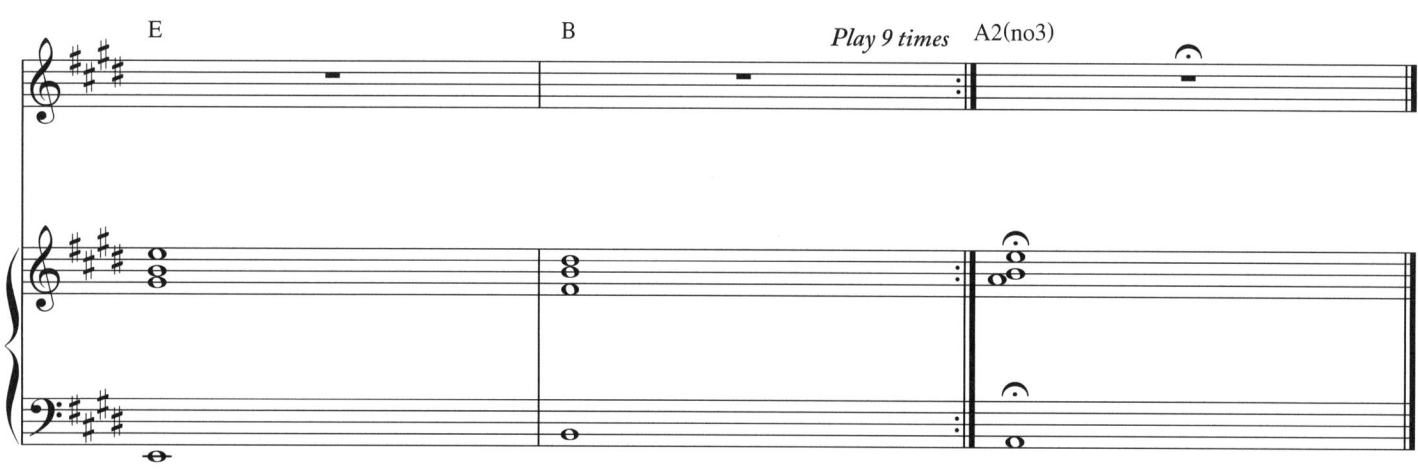
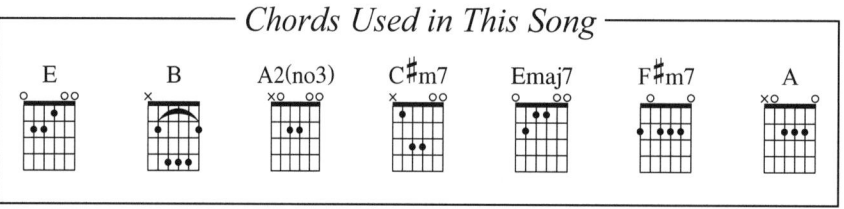